THE
QUICKSAND
BOOK

*Special thanks to Saebyul Choe
and Thomas Trombone,
American Museum of Natural History*

Tomie dePaola's

# THE QUICKSAND BOOK

Holiday House · New York

For "Stevem"
& his grandmother

Well, don't worry. It just so happens that I know a lot about quicksand. So look and listen carefully. It will be very interesting, and you might learn something.

First of all, quicksand is not a special kind of sand. It is plain sand. But when water is forced upward through the sand, the grains are pushed apart and the sand swells. When this happens, the sand is no longer firm and cannot support heavy weight. That is why you are sinking.

You see, when you struggle you push more quicksand out of the way and sink faster. I've noticed that most people, if they stay calm, only sink up to their necks. If you had fallen on your back, you could have floated on top of it, the same way you can float on the Great Salt Lake or the Dead Sea. But it's a little late for that now.

Do you know where quicksand can be found? No? Well, I'll tell you. The most common form of quicksand is found along the shores and in the beds of slow rivers and streams that have underground springs, just like where you are.

QUICKSAND WILL FORM ALONG SHORES OR UNDER WATER NEAR A BANK.

WATER

←SPRINGS→ QUICKSAND ←SPRINGS→

ROCK

QUICKSAND WILL SOMETIMES FORM IN MIDSTREAM.

THE SUN BAKES A THIN CRUST ON THE SAND.

ROCK QUICKSAND WATER

SPRING

QUICKSAND CAN FORM IN A RIVERBED THAT LOOKS DRY.

THERE IS A THIN CRUST HERE, TOO.
↓

ROCK QUICKSAND

SPRING

In just a minute. I want you to look at what happens to animals if they happen to wander into quicksand.

HORSES USUALLY LEAP OUT IN SHORT RABBIT-LIKE JUMPS.

MULES LIE DOWN ON THEIR BELLIES WITH THEIR FEET TUCKED UNDERNEATH THEM. THEY WON'T SINK IN THIS POSITION.

CATTLE NEED HELP BECAUSE THEY PANIC AND SINK QUICKLY.

Jungle Boy!
I'm up to my shoulders.
Help me out!

If you had been carrying a stick or a pole, you could have gotten out like this. Read the chart carefully. These facts are very helpful if you are alone . . . and if you have a stick with you.

① CALL FOR HELP.

② FALL ON YOUR BACK.

③ PUT STICK UNDER SHOULDERS WITH ARMS OUT TO SIDE.

④ PUSH STICK TO HIPS.

⑤ SLOWLY PULL LEGS OUT ONE AT A TIME.

⑥ DON'T TIRE YOURSELF OUT - TAKE RESTS BETWEEN MOVES.

⑦ USE THE STICK TO KEEP "FLOATING" ON QUICKSAND.

⑧ ROLL A LITTLE AT A TIME TO SOLID GROUND.

⑨ REST.

But, Jungle Girl, this is your lucky day. I'm here to help you. I could stretch out on that log and pull you out with my hands. That would take a lot of work. Instead, I shall use a strong vine. Slip the vine under your arms and hang on.

You're welcome. Next time, don't be so careless and watch where you're going.

# How To Make Your Own Quicksand

1. MAKE A HOLE IN THE BOTTOM OF A PAIL.

2. STICK A HOSE UP THROUGH THE HOLE AND MAKE IT WATERTIGHT.

3. FILL THE PAIL 3/4 FULL WITH SAND.

4. PLACE A HEAVY OBJECT ON TOP OF THE SAND. THE OBJECT WILL STAY PUT.

5. TURN ON THE HOSE SO THAT A LITTLE WATER TRICKLES UP THROUGH THE SAND. THE SAND WILL SWELL AND GRAINS WILL PULL APART. WHEN THERE IS ENOUGH WATER TO MAKE THE SAND "QUICK," THE OBJECT WILL SINK.

6. TURN OFF THE WATER. THE SAND WILL SETTLE AND WATER WILL COME TO THE TOP. THE SAND CAN NOW HOLD ANOTHER HEAVY OBJECT. THIS IS BECAUSE THE WATER IS SQUEEZED TOWARD THE TOP, AND THE GRAINS OF SAND AREN'T PULLED APART AS MUCH.